Presented to

....

on the occasion of

....

With love from

....

Lion Publishing
1705 Hubbard Avenue, Batavia, Illinois 60510, USA
ISBN 0 7459 2398 4

First edition 1993

Library of Congress Cataloging-In-Publication Data
Hathaway, Mary
  Celebrating marriage / Mary Hathaway
  ISBN 0-7459-2398-4
  1. Marriage Religious aspects Christianity.
  2. Marriage Biblical teaching. 3. Marriage
Poetry. I. Title
BV4596.M3H38 1993 92-38553
242'.644 dc20 CIP

Printed and bound in Malaysia

Acknowledgments
Photographs by Neil Beer: pages 7 and 16, 28/29, 42;
Ebenezer Pictures: page 19; David Kemp: page 17 (top);
Lion Publishing: pages 10, 15, 17 (bottom), 32, 45;
Willi Rauch: pages 14/15, 34/35, 44; Spices/ Nelson
Hargreaves: page 31; ZEFA: pages 11, 12, 12/13,
18/19, 20, 21, 22/23, 23, 24, 24/25, 26, 27, 30/31,
32/33, 35, 36, 36/37, 38, 39, 40, 40/41, 43, endpapers

CELEBRATING MARRIAGE

Mary Hathaway

A LION BOOK
Oxford · Batavia · Sydney

INTRODUCTION

I believe in marriage. I believe it was God's idea and that he meant it for good for both the woman and the man. If this is not how it works out, then it is the way we handle it that is wrong, not the idea in the first place. So what did God intend marriage to be?

This was the question I asked myself at the beginning of my own married life because it seemed to me that many found marriage to be a negative thing, a lack of freedom, the taking on of unwelcome responsibilities or even the loss of identity.

Finding the answer has led me on a long quest. The first thing I learned was that love has to grow. You don't plant an acorn today and expect to see an oak tree tomorrow! Then I found that marriage is hard work. It costs—like anything else worth having. I decided that I expected too much of marriage, too quickly, and that it is normal to have problems. It's what you do with those problems that matters.

But more and more I began to realize what a precious and beautiful gift this special relationship is. One of the greatest forces for good in the world is the love between a man and a woman in marriage, as God intended it to be.

In this book you will find some of the discoveries I have made in a quest that is still going on.

Mary Hathaway
February 1992

*M*arriage is given,
that husband and wife may comfort and
help each other,
living faithfully together
in need and in plenty,
in sorrow and in joy.

It is given,
that with delight and tenderness
they may know each other in love,
and, through the joy of their bodily union,
may strengthen the union
of their hearts and lives.

ALTERNATIVE SERVICE BOOK

F ALLING IN LOVE

How beautiful you are, my love;
how your eyes shine with love!
Like a lily among thorns
is my darling among women.

SONG OF SOLOMON 1:15, 2:2

Like an apple-tree among the trees of the forest,
So is my dearest compared to other men.
I love to sit in its shadow and its fruit is sweet to my taste.
He brought me to his banqueting hall
and raised the banner of love over me.

SONG OF SOLOMON 2:3,4

Fall night

Edged with misty darkness
the vast dome of the sky
wrapped us in the spacious
stillness of the night.

Along with the stars
and hand in hand, we stood
between the marshes
and the sea,
and looked down upon
the wreaths of mist
cold yet incandescent
in the silver light.

Here and there
the silent pools
gleamed through
and we saw
the quivering path
traced by the full moon
across the water
and listened to the waves
pounding on the shore.

And as we walked
within the beauty
of the fall night,
God held you and me
and the stars
in the palm of his hand.

December sun

The air was soft
and mellow for December.
We walked by the lake
through the wetness
of the autumn woods
together,
both of us thirsty
for quietness.

Sitting on a fallen tree
we watched the herons
and were dazzled
by the brightness of the sun
across the water.
Hardly a word
passed between us.

And then we parted,
only for an hour or so.
But the world went cold
just for a moment
and a shadow stole
across the morning.

For as I turned
away from you,
I had to break
the fine spun
threads of light
our love had made
between us.

And once broken
I knew that special moment
would be gone for ever,
drifting away beyond
our reach to melt
into the December sun.

Summer gold

My lover is mine and I am his.

SONG OF SOLOMON 2:16

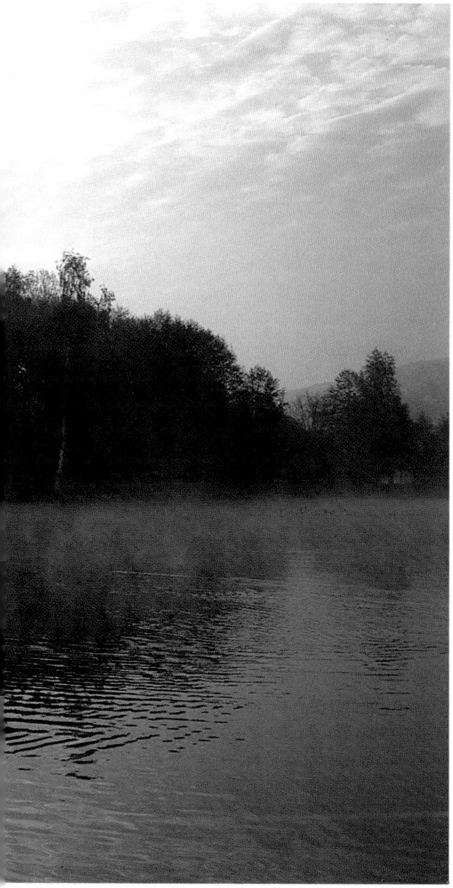

Reflections
from the branches
of the willow tree
and two white swans.

Flowers
like tiny jewels,
fringing the edges
of the water.

Grass heads
gently swaying,
translucent
in the evening sun.

Haziness
of distant hills,
blond stubbled
due for ploughing.

Companionship
of love at ease
and the joy
of hearts contented.

Golden dust
spread over all
from the summer
safely gathered.

Marriage is to be honored by all.

HEBREWS 13:4

The Lord God said, 'It is not good
for the man to live alone.'

GENESIS 2:18

A man will leave his father and
mother and unite with his wife and
the two will become one.

EPHESIANS 5:31

In praise of marriage

Marriage is a threefold cord,
the love of husband, wife and God
entwined together makes it
tough and durable.

Marriage is a musical instrument
where each string
retains its own note and yet
quivers with the same melody.

Marriage is a garden
where each plant has space
to change and mature and within it
is set free to find fulfillment.

Marriage is a harbor,
somewhere to shelter from the storm
and to return to with gladness
after voyaging on the high seas.

Marriage is a place of sanctuary,
the home of peace and safety
where people can be renewed
and healed from the wounds of life.

Marriage is a sapling
that grows into a leafy tree
and many are glad
of the shade of its love.

So God made marriage
to be both strong and beautiful
and to be a source of blessing
to all the world.

17

C OMMITMENT

I take you...
to have and told
from this day forward;
for better, for worse,
for richer, for poorer,
in sickness and in health,
to love and to cherish,
till death us do part.

With my body I honor you,
all that I am I give to you,
and all that I have I share with you.
Within the love of God,
Father, Son and Holy Spirit.

THE ALTERNATIVE SERVICE
BOOK

Man must not separate...
what God has joined together.

MATTHEW 19:6

You alone have I loved

You alone have I loved. You said at the beginning not just that you were in love with me, but that you were determined to love me. For you knew that love on its own is a fickle thing. It is only when it is rooted in the will that it can ride out the storms of life.

You knew that the way might be hard, that the sacrifices made might have to be unequal, that at times, even the feelings of love you had towards me might well disappear. And yet, with God's help, you were determined to love me to the end.

And so once again I pledge myself to you, for where else can I go to find such a love as this? For you only have I loved from the beginning, and with God's help, so it shall be until the ending of my days.

Love's touch

Lord, take my hands
and fill them
with your beauty
when I touch him.
Let love and joy,
laughter and healing,
comfort and belonging
flow from my hands
into his body and on
into his spirit
that he may be
lifted and enriched.

Weave my caresses
into a garment
of warmth and light
that he can wear
as he goes out
into the world.
And let all
the loveliness of heaven
be in my hands
as they move
to touch him with love.

Close your heart to every love but mine;
hold no one in your arms but me.
Love is as powerful as death;
passion is as strong as death itself.

It bursts into flame
and burns like a raging fire.
Water cannot put it out;
no flood can drown it.

SONG OF SOLOMON 8:6, 7

Two families united

By this marriage our two families have been united. May all of us and particularly the parents of the bride and groom increase in affection for one another, and find in one another a source of help and strength.

May we learn to value the ideals and beliefs of others. May the love and understanding of our families bring nearer the day Christ prayed for, when there shall be only one flock and one shepherd.

We pray for the friends of [the bride and groom]. We pray especially for those who have had some part in bringing them to this happy day. May God bless them with the gift of his own undying friendship.

NATIONAL LITURGICAL
COMMISSION OF ENGLAND AND WALES

Two are better off than one,
because they can work together more
effectively. If one of them falls down,
the other can help him up.

ECCLESIASTES 4:9, 10

The gift of marriage

Lord, marriage is your gift to us,
not something to be taken for granted.
So we ask that you will help us
in our relationship together
as man and wife.

Help us to respect each other
and to be aware that we are
both equally important to you.
Help us not to complain that one
works harder than the other,
but to make the effort
to see each other's point of view.

Let there be frankness with tenderness,
patience with a sense of humor
and the ability to admit
that once in a while we could be wrong.

And let us be willing
to share our happiness with others
by opening our home to them
and having time for their joys and sorrows
as well as our own.

Men and women

God made men and women to build each other up and bring out the best in each other. He wanted them both to find complete fulfillment, separately and together. And marriage was to be a relationship of real love, the sort that sets people free to be themselves, where a man and a woman could respect each other equally and work together in harmony.

So what has gone wrong? Everywhere men and women are in competition. They tear one another down instead of building one another up. We are all guilty of hurting each other, and it must hurt God as well.

So, Lord, I bring to you all the women who have been hurt by men and all the men who have been hurt by women, and ask that you may make them whole. I ask that in our own marriage we may grow in respect for one another so that it may become the beautiful gift you intended. Help us, in our generation, to show something of marriage as you meant it to be, where love leads to liberation of the mind and spirit. And in seeking the healing of our own attitudes, let us begin the healing of the world.

Prayer for a new home

Lord, help us in our home
and let us always be thankful for it.

May all the work here be done out of love,
love of you and love for others,
the washing up, the cleaning,
the cooking, the decorating,
done with the knowledge
that you are always here.

Help us in the secret places of our home
where no one else sees except you,
where we show what we can be like—
bad-tempered, depressed, irritable—
that even there your love may be in control.
And may we be tender-hearted,
forgiving one another, even as you forgive us.

We ask that every room of our home
may be filled with your presence,
and that each room may be restful,
pleasing to look at, and relaxing to be in:

not so clean that it makes people feel uncomfortable
and not so untidy that it looks uncared for.

Let it be a place where people feel welcomed
and loved
and go out feeling blessed.

Homes are built on the
foundation of wisdom and
understanding. Where there is
knowledge the rooms are
furnished with valuable,
beautiful things.

PROVERBS 24:3, 4

Homes are made
by the wisdom
of women.

PROVERBS 14:1

A flower of light

A home is
a flower of light,
blossoming in the dark.

A home is
a circle of flame,
glowing in the cold.

A home is
four walls enfolding,
protecting from the storm.

A home is
a precious gift,
to be received with thanksgiving.

I gave you light

I gave you light
and now your brightness
streams past mine
and I am in your shadow.

Yet gladly am I
eclipsed by you,
for your light kindles mine,
letting it grow
so that one day
it will equal yours.

Then yours will dim
and borrow strength from mine,
both of us growing
in the light
we give each other.

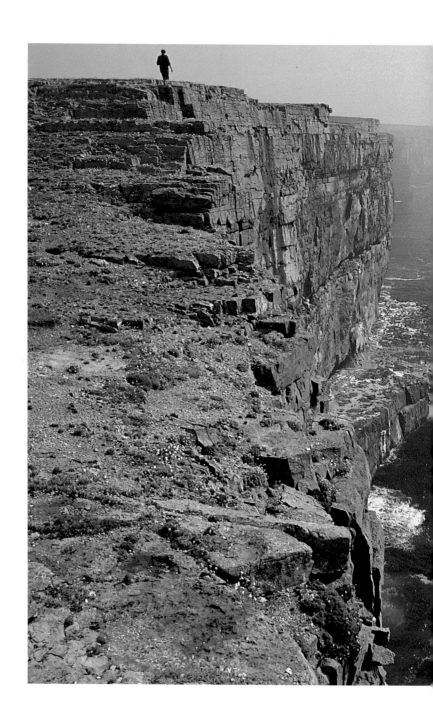

The wells of silence

I am glad to find the wells of silence again within me, to find joy in being alone and unafraid. When I am surrounded by noise, people and pressure, then I secretly long to draw deeply from them.

I have not yet learned how to do that. But I thank God that the depths of solitude are limited by your love. Now there is much greater joy in being alone, because I know you are coming back to me.

Furnished with love

Houses are made with bricks and mortar,
homes are made with happy relationships.

Houses are filled with household goods,
homes are filled with understanding and forgiveness.

Houses are used for people to live in,
homes are used to train people for life.

Thank you, God, for houses that are homes.
Bless each home so that it may be furnished with love.

Father of all, make the
roof of my house wide
enough for all opinions,
oil the door of my house
so it opens easily to
friend and stranger and
set such a table in my
house that my whole
family may speak kindly
and freely around it.

PRAYER FROM HAWAII

The Bible does not say very much about homes; it
says a great deal about the things that make them. It
speaks about life and love and joy and peace and rest.
If we get a house and put these into it, we shall have
secured a home.

JOHN HENRY JOWETT

31

You were there

You were there—
and to see your face
was like laughter
in a silent place.

You were there—
and your presence near
was like starlight
in a cloud of fear.

You were there—
when my strength was through
I went on giving
as I took from you.

You were there—
when hours seemed like years
and I had passed long since
the place for tears.

You were there—
in a sea of sand
like one stable point,
I felt your hand.

Now I know
just how much you care.
When I most needed you
—you were there.

The candle of love

Lord, when this candle of love
becomes too heavy
for my hands to carry,
thank you that you will take it
into your strong ones.

For Lord, you know
how precious it is to me
and how much I care
that it should not go out.

Shadows and sunshine

Light gives
shape
to darkness
and darkness
to light.

For light
on its own
is formless
unless bordered
by shadow
and darkness
that is total,
has no boundaries
and overwhelms
the spirit.

But shadows
and sunshine
together
make shapes
that are beautiful
in the pattern
of the whole.

This enemy of love

Deliver me from resentment, Lord,
for resentment lives by eating love.
Hideous, loathsome, alive,
it creeps insidiously into
the depths of our beings,
quietly, subconsciously,
careful not to give itself a name.

Open hatred is sad
but it knows what it is.
Resentment disguises itself
so that gradually
it becomes acceptable.

Resentment and love
cannot live together;
one pushes the other out
and one root of bitterness
can destroy a life's work of loving.

So, Lord, help me to watch
and help me to pray,
and set me free from this
enemy of love.

The start of an argument is like the first break in a dam; stop before it goes any further.

PROVERBS 17:14

Remembering wrongs can break up a friendship.

PROVERBS 5:20

Be kind and tender-hearted to one
another, and forgive one another, as
God has forgiven you through Christ.

EPHESIANS 4:32

Be careful how you think,
your life is shaped by your thoughts.

PROVERBS 4:23

Each day I will give thanks

I will try
always to think well of you,
for though I love you
there will be times
when I do not like you.

So I need to watch
that any resentful thoughts
I may have about you
are not allowed to stay in my mind.
For, given enough time,
just one bruised apple
can turn all the rest bad.

So I will try
to let my mind dwell
on the special moments of happiness
that we share together
and each day I will give thanks
for all that I love in you
and the joy
you have brought into my life.

CHILDREN

The gift of children

Children are a gift from God.
May we always be thankful for them—
even when they tax our patience
to the uttermost!

May we never take them for granted
but be grateful
that they have been entrusted
to our care.

As we respect them
so may they respect us.
Let our discipline be wise
and our authority worthy of their trust.
Let there be laughter and fun
as we enjoy being together,
not complaining of our responsibilities,
but able to grasp firmly
every joy that goes with them.

We pray for this couple, that in their marriage all your will for them may be fulfilled; bestow upon them the gift and heritage of children; and endue them with all the gifts and graces needed for wise parenthood; through Jesus Christ our Lord. Amen.

THE METHODIST SERVICE BOOK

It [marriage] is given, that they might have children and be blessed in caring for them and bringing them up in accordance with God's will, to his praise and glory.

THE ALTERNATIVE
SERVICE BOOK

Children are a gift from the Lord;
they are a real blessing.

PSALM 127:3

Circle of love

Circle of safety
in adventure,

circle of warmth
in the cold,

circle of life
in drought,

circle of belonging
in loneliness,

circle of trust
in uncertainty,

circle of gladness
in joy,

circle of love
in your arms
at the end of the day.

My soul takes pleasure in three things
and they are beautiful in the sight of
the Lord and of men . . . a husband and
wife who live in harmony.

SIRACH 25:1

A faithful friend is a sturdy shelter,
he that has found one has found a treasure.

There is nothing so precious as a faithful
friend,
and no scales can measure his excellence.

A faithful friend is an elixir of life.

SIRACH 6:14–16

The anniversary

I will come back here
with you, my love,
and there will be a moon
and a thousand stars
and I will sit with you
and watch the black velvet
of the mountains
and listen to the night.

We will talk quietly,
looking back over the long years,
with children grown up
and all the joys and sorrows
that have passed between
then and now.

And I will give thanks
for all that you
have been to me,
lover and confidant,
adviser, protector and companion.

But most of all
I pray that the hand
that holds mine
may still be then,
as it is now,
the hand of my dearest friend.

GROWING OLD TOGETHER

My lover knows that with him I find
contentment and peace.

SONG OF SOLOMON 8:16

Lord, I would like us
to grow old together;

to enjoy having children
and yet to be content
for them to leave home;

to be busy
and yet not too busy
to make time for each other;

to make love
that grows younger
with bodies that grow older;

to have joy
that looks forwards
and not backwards;

and most of all,
to hold each other
in reverent hands.

Love is eternal.
Meanwhile these three remain:
faith, hope, love; and the greatest
of these is love.

I CORINTHIANS 13:8, 13

Grow old along with me!
The best is yet to be,
The last of life for which the first was made.
Our times are in His hand
Who saith, 'A whole I planned,'
Youth shows but half; trust God; see all,
Nor be afraid.

ROBERT BROWNING

G OD'S   SPECIAL   GIFT

The parable of the apple tree

Once there was a man and a woman and, as well as giving them to each other, God also gave them a gift to share, which he called a special way of loving.

At first they found it unbelievably beautiful. They longed to please each other and only saw the fine, the good and the best in the other person. Then gradually they were aware that things had changed. They began to find fault with each other, now and then at first but then, it seemed, constantly. They were always tired with just keeping up with the responsibilities of having a home and family,  and they feared they had lost the love they once had. But they plodded on and gradually found a safety and a satisfaction in each other that went much deeper than the love they had in the early days. They found support in each other, as they shared the ups and down of living, and their children and those that shared their home were glad of the shelter of this love.

And so the years went by and one by one the children left home, and the man and the woman grew older and sometimes felt very tired. They had shared a lifetime of joys and sorrows but at times they felt so alone.

'Have we been what you wanted us to be? Have we done what you wanted us to do with this special way of loving?' they asked their Maker one day.

He came and stood beside them and spoke gently: 'Listen to the parable of the apple tree.

'Your first love for each other was like the blossom on the apple tree. It was very beautiful but it could not last. Many people think this is the only part of loving and when the blossom falls they will not seek a deeper love, but go like butterflies from flower to flower and are never satisfied. You came through this to find shade and shelter during the long summer. So your love made a safe place for your children to grow up in and gave joy to those who passed through your home. This part of love is very hard work and it is good to stop and remember that the fruit is growing steadily, hidden among the leaves, though at the time you are often not aware of it.

'When the children left home and life became a little less demanding, at first you felt lonely and rather lost. But you had taken care of your love for each other during the long years of busyness and together you found a new and deeper friendship. You did not find yourselves facing each other like strangers when the children had gone, as many do. You were able to give a tenderness and depth of understanding to each other that far outshone the beauty of your first love as the fruit of the apple tree outshines the blossom.

'Your children and those who have passed through your home are the precious seeds of love. It is only when the fruit leaves the tree that the seeds inside are free to fulfill all their potential. As the seeds in the apple will never be able to germinate and grow into new trees unless they fall from the branches, so it is only as you let your children go that they are able to love fully, and your love for them is perfected.

'You are most beautiful in my eyes, for you have shown all the world what I meant this special way of loving to be. You have seen it through from its first beauty to the fullness of joy and from you the seeds of love have gone down to new generations. So few endure to this stage where their love can grow to this maturity. The blossom of the apple tree does not last and neither do the leaves. Only the fruit gives the seeds of love which can be passed on. It is only those who do not give up who reach the joy of harvest. So your love is passed on from generation to generation like a chain of light stretching into eternity.'

And the man and the woman were glad, and held the outstretched hands of their Maker. And then it was that they saw that not only his hands, but theirs also, were scarred with love, and as they looked at each other in joy and wonder, the light of heaven bathed them in glory.

And the name of the special way of loving that God gave to the man and the woman was—marriage.